CONTENTS

Barcode Scanner

Expense Tracker

Weather Application

Note-taking App

Task Scheduler

Countdown Timer

Chess Game

Binary Converter

Morse Code Translator

Budget Planner

Word Counter

Image Slider

File Compressor/Decompressor

Recipe Manager

Movie Database

Student Grade Tracker

Password Generator

Music Playlist Manager

Countdown to Events

Personal Diary

Morse Code Generator

Address Book with Database

Library Management System

Text Encryption/Decryption

Barcode Generator

Pomodoro Timer

Hello World Program in C#

```csharp
using System;
class HelloWorld
{
    static void Main()
    {
        Console.WriteLine("Hello, world!");
    }
}
```

Calculator Program in C#

```csharp
using System;
class Calculator
{
    static void Main()
    {
        double num1, num2, result;
        char op;
        Console.Write("Enter first number: ");
        num1 = Convert.ToDouble(Console.ReadLine());
        Console.Write("Enter operator (+, -, *, /): ");
        op = Convert.ToChar(Console.ReadLine());
        Console.Write("Enter second number: ");
        num2 = Convert.ToDouble(Console.ReadLine());
        switch (op)
        {
            case '+':
                result = num1 + num2;
                break;
            case '-':
                result = num1 - num2;
```

```csharp
            break;
        case '*':
            result = num1 * num2;
            break;
        case '/':
            if (num2 != 0)
                result = num1 / num2;
            else
            {
                Console.WriteLine("Error: Division by zero.");
                return;
            }
            break;
        default:
            Console.WriteLine("Error: Invalid operator.");
            return;
    }
    Console.WriteLine("Result: " + result);
  }
}
```

Temperature Converter Program in C#

```csharp
using System;
class TemperatureConverter
{
    static void Main()
    {
        double fahrenheit, celsius;
        Console.Write("Enter temperature in Fahrenheit: ");
        fahrenheit = Convert.ToDouble(Console.ReadLine());
        celsius = (fahrenheit - 32) * 5 / 9;
```

```
    Console.WriteLine("Temperature in Celsius: " + celsius);
  }
}
```

BMI Calculator Program in C#

```
using System;
class BMICalculator
{
   static void Main()
   {
      double weight, height, bmi;
      Console.Write("Enter weight in kilograms: ");
      weight = Convert.ToDouble(Console.ReadLine());
      Console.Write("Enter height in meters: ");
      height = Convert.ToDouble(Console.ReadLine());
      bmi = weight / (height * height);
      Console.WriteLine("BMI: " + bmi);
   }
}
```

Simple Stopwatch Program in C#

```
using System;
using System.Threading;
class SimpleStopwatch
{
   static void Main()
   {
      int seconds = 0;
      while (true)
      {
         Console.WriteLine("Elapsed time: " + seconds + " seconds");
```

Mastering Practical C-Sharp Programming

```csharp
        Thread.Sleep(1000);

        seconds++;

    }

  }

}
```

Alarm Clock Program in C#

```csharp
using System;
using System.Threading;
class AlarmClock
{
    static void Main()
    {
        Console.Write("Enter the number of minutes for the alarm: ");
        int minutes = Convert.ToInt32(Console.ReadLine());
        int seconds = minutes * 60;
        Console.WriteLine("Alarm set for " + minutes + " minutes.");
        Thread.Sleep(seconds * 1000);
        Console.WriteLine("Time's up! Alarm triggered.");
    }
}
```

Tic Tac Toe Game Program in C#

```csharp
using System;
class TicTacToe
{
    static char[,] board = new char[3, 3];
    static char currentPlayer = 'X';

    static void Main()
    {
```

```csharp
        InitializeBoard();

        PrintBoard();

        while (!IsGameOver())
        {
            PlayMove();
            PrintBoard();
            ChangePlayer();
        }

        char winner = GetWinner();
        if (winner == ' ')
            Console.WriteLine("It's a draw!");
        else
            Console.WriteLine("Player " + winner + " wins!");
    }

    static void InitializeBoard()
    {
        for (int i = 0; i < 3; i++)
        {
            for (int j = 0; j < 3; j++)
            {
                board[i, j] = ' ';
            }
        }
    }

    static void PrintBoard()
    {
        Console.WriteLine("  0 1 2");
```

```csharp
    for (int i = 0; i < 3; i++)
    {
        Console.Write(i + " ");
        for (int j = 0; j < 3; j++)
        {
            Console.Write(board[i, j] + " ");
        }
        Console.WriteLine();
    }
}


static void PlayMove()
{
    int row, col;
    do
    {
        Console.Write("Player " + currentPlayer + ", enter row and column: ");
        string[] input = Console.ReadLine().Split();
        row = int.Parse(input[0]);
        col = int.Parse(input[1]);
    } while (!IsValidMove(row, col));

    board[row, col] = currentPlayer;
}


static bool IsValidMove(int row, int col)
{
    if (row < 0 || row >= 3 || col < 0 || col >= 3 || board[row, col] != ' ')
        return false;
    return true;
}
```

```csharp
static void ChangePlayer()
{
    currentPlayer = (currentPlayer == 'X') ? 'O' : 'X';
}


static bool IsGameOver()
{
    if (GetWinner() != ' ' || IsBoardFull())
        return true;
    return false;
}


static char GetWinner()
{
    // Check rows
    for (int i = 0; i < 3; i++)
    {
        if (board[i, 0] == board[i, 1] && board[i, 1] == board[i, 2] && board[i, 0] != ' ')
            return board[i, 0];
    }


    // Check columns
    for (int i = 0; i < 3; i++)
    {
        if (board[0, i] == board[1, i] && board[1, i] == board[2, i] && board[0, i] != ' ')
            return board[0, i];
    }


    // Check diagonals
```

```csharp
        if ((board[0, 0] == board[1, 1] && board[1, 1] == board[2, 2] && board[0, 0] != ' ')
||
            (board[0, 2] == board[1, 1] && board[1, 1] == board[2, 0] && board[0, 2] != ' '))
            return board[1, 1];

        return ' ';
    }


    static bool IsBoardFull()
    {
        for (int i = 0; i < 3; i++)
        {
            for (int j = 0; j < 3; j++)
            {
                if (board[i, j] == ' ')
                    return false;
            }
        }
        return true;
    }
}
```

To-Do List Application Program in C#

```csharp
using System;
using System.Collections.Generic;
class ToDoList
{
    static List<string> tasks = new List<string>();
    static void Main()
    {
        while (true)
```

```csharp
        {
            Console.WriteLine("1. Add Task");
            Console.WriteLine("2. View Tasks");
            Console.WriteLine("3. Exit");
            Console.Write("Enter your choice: ");
            int choice = Convert.ToInt32(Console.ReadLine());
            switch (choice)
            {
                case 1:
                    AddTask();
                    break;
                case 2:
                    ViewTasks();
                    break;
                case 3:
                    return;
                default:
                    Console.WriteLine("Invalid choice. Please try again.");
                    break;
            }
        }
    }
    static void AddTask()
    {
        Console.Write("Enter task: ");
        string task = Console.ReadLine();
        tasks.Add(task);
        Console.WriteLine("Task added successfully.");
    }
    static void ViewTasks()
    {
```

```
        if (tasks.Count == 0)
        {
            Console.WriteLine("No tasks found.");
            return;
        }
        Console.WriteLine("Tasks:");
        for (int i = 0; i < tasks.Count; i++)
        {
            Console.WriteLine((i + 1) + ". " + tasks[i]);
        }
    }
}
```

Simple Text Editor Program in C#

```
using System;
using System.IO;
class SimpleTextEditor
{
    static void Main()
    {
        string fileName = "text.txt";

        Console.WriteLine("Simple Text Editor");
        Console.WriteLine("1. Create New File");
        Console.WriteLine("2. Open Existing File");
        Console.Write("Enter your choice: ");
        int choice = Convert.ToInt32(Console.ReadLine());

        switch (choice)
        {
            case 1:
```

```csharp
            CreateNewFile(fileName);

            break;

        case 2:

            OpenExistingFile(fileName);

            break;

        default:

            Console.WriteLine("Invalid choice.");

            break;

    }

}

static void CreateNewFile(string fileName)

{

    Console.Write("Enter text: ");

    string text = Console.ReadLine();

    try

    {

        File.WriteAllText(fileName, text);

        Console.WriteLine("File created successfully.");

    }

    catch (Exception ex)

    {

        Console.WriteLine("Error: " + ex.Message);

    }

}

static void OpenExistingFile(string fileName)

{

    try

    {

        string text = File.ReadAllText(fileName);

        Console.WriteLine("File content:");

        Console.WriteLine(text);
```

```csharp
        }
        catch (FileNotFoundException)
        {
            Console.WriteLine("Error: File not found.");
        }
        catch (Exception ex)
        {
            Console.WriteLine("Error: " + ex.Message);
        }
    }
}
```

Currency Converter Program in C#

```csharp
using System;
class CurrencyConverter
{
    static void Main()
    {
        double amount, convertedAmount;
        string fromCurrency, toCurrency;

        Console.Write("Enter amount: ");
        amount = Convert.ToDouble(Console.ReadLine());

        Console.Write("Enter from currency (e.g., USD, EUR): ");
        fromCurrency = Console.ReadLine().ToUpper();

        Console.Write("Enter to currency (e.g., USD, EUR): ");
        toCurrency = Console.ReadLine().ToUpper();

        convertedAmount = ConvertCurrency(amount, fromCurrency, toCurrency);
```

```csharp
        Console.WriteLine("Converted amount: " + convertedAmount + " " + toCurrency);
    }


    static double ConvertCurrency(double amount, string fromCurrency, string
toCurrency)
    {
        // Conversion rates for demonstration purposes
        double usdToEur = 0.85;
        double usdToGbp = 0.72;
        double eurToUsd = 1.18;
        double gbpToUsd = 1.38;

        double convertedAmount = 0;

        if (fromCurrency == "USD" && toCurrency == "EUR")
            convertedAmount = amount * usdToEur;
        else if (fromCurrency == "USD" && toCurrency == "GBP")
            convertedAmount = amount * usdToGbp;
        else if (fromCurrency == "EUR" && toCurrency == "USD")
            convertedAmount = amount * eurToUsd;
        else if (fromCurrency == "GBP" && toCurrency == "USD")
            convertedAmount = amount * gbpToUsd;
        else
            Console.WriteLine("Conversion not supported.");

        return convertedAmount;
    }
}
```

Guess the Number Game Program in C#

Mastering Practical C-Sharp Programming

```csharp
using System;
class GuessTheNumber
{
    static void Main()
    {
        Random random = new Random();
        int secretNumber = random.Next(1, 101);
        int guess;
        int attempts = 0;
        Console.WriteLine("Welcome to Guess the Number Game!");
        do
        {
            Console.Write("Enter your guess (1-100): ");
            guess = Convert.ToInt32(Console.ReadLine());
            attempts++;

            if (guess < secretNumber)
                Console.WriteLine("Too low! Try again.");
            else if (guess > secretNumber)
                Console.WriteLine("Too high! Try again.");
            else
                Console.WriteLine("Congratulations! You guessed the number in " + attempts
+ " attempts.");
        } while (guess != secretNumber);
    }
}
```

File Explorer Program in C#

```csharp
using System;
using System.IO;
```

Mastering Practical C-Sharp Programming

```csharp
class FileExplorer
{
    static void Main()
    {
        Console.WriteLine("File Explorer");
        Console.WriteLine("1. List Files in Directory");
        Console.WriteLine("2. Display File Content");
        Console.Write("Enter your choice: ");
        int choice = Convert.ToInt32(Console.ReadLine());
        switch (choice)
        {
            case 1:
                ListFiles();
                break;
            case 2:
                DisplayFileContent();
                break;
            default:
                Console.WriteLine("Invalid choice.");
                break;
        }
    }
    static void ListFiles()
    {
        Console.Write("Enter directory path: ");
        string directoryPath = Console.ReadLine();

        try
        {
            string[] files = Directory.GetFiles(directoryPath);
            Console.WriteLine("Files in directory:");
```

```csharp
        foreach (string file in files)
        {
            Console.WriteLine(Path.GetFileName(file));
        }
    }
    catch (Exception ex)
    {
        Console.WriteLine("Error: " + ex.Message);
    }
}
static void DisplayFileContent()
{
    Console.Write("Enter file path: ");
    string filePath = Console.ReadLine();
    try
    {
        string content = File.ReadAllText(filePath);
        Console.WriteLine("File content:");
        Console.WriteLine(content);
    }
    catch (FileNotFoundException)
    {
        Console.WriteLine("Error: File not found.");
    }
    catch (Exception ex)
    {
        Console.WriteLine("Error: " + ex.Message);
    }
}
}
```

Basic Calculator with GUI Program in C#

```csharp
using System;
using System.Windows.Forms;
class BasicCalculatorGUI : Form
{
    private TextBox txtNumber1;
    private TextBox txtNumber2;
    private Button btnAdd;
    private Button btnSubtract;
    private Button btnMultiply;
    private Button btnDivide;
    private Label lblResult;

    public BasicCalculatorGUI()
    {
        InitializeComponent();
    }

    private void InitializeComponent()
    {
        this.txtNumber1 = new TextBox();
        this.txtNumber2 = new TextBox();
        this.btnAdd = new Button();
        this.btnSubtract = new Button();
        this.btnMultiply = new Button();
        this.btnDivide = new Button();
        this.lblResult = new Label();
        this.SuspendLayout();
        //
        // txtNumber1
        //
```

```csharp
            this.txtNumber1.Location = new System.Drawing.Point(30, 30);

            this.txtNumber1.Name = "txtNumber1";

            this.txtNumber1.Size = new System.Drawing.Size(100, 20);

            this.txtNumber1.TabIndex = 0;

            //

            // txtNumber2

            //

            this.txtNumber2.Location = new System.Drawing.Point(30, 70);

            this.txtNumber2.Name = "txtNumber2";

            this.txtNumber2.Size = new System.Drawing.Size(100, 20);

            this.txtNumber2.TabIndex = 1;

            //

            // btnAdd

            //

            this.btnAdd.Location = new System.Drawing.Point(30, 110);

            this.btnAdd.Name = "btnAdd";

            this.btnAdd.Size = new System.Drawing.Size(40, 40);

            this.btnAdd.TabIndex = 2;

            this.btnAdd.Text = "+";

            this.btnAdd.UseVisualStyleBackColor = true;

            this.btnAdd.Click += new System.EventHandler(this.btnAdd_Click);

            //

            // btnSubtract

            //

            this.btnSubtract.Location = new System.Drawing.Point(80, 110);

            this.btnSubtract.Name = "btnSubtract";

            this.btnSubtract.Size = new System.Drawing.Size(40, 40);

            this.btnSubtract.TabIndex = 3;

            this.btnSubtract.Text = "-";

            this.btnSubtract.UseVisualStyleBackColor = true;

            this.btnSubtract.Click += new System.EventHandler(this.btnSubtract_Click);
```

```
//
// btnMultiply
//
this.btnMultiply.Location = new System.Drawing.Point(30, 160);
this.btnMultiply.Name = "btnMultiply";
this.btnMultiply.Size = new System.Drawing.Size(40, 40);
this.btnMultiply.TabIndex = 4;
this.btnMultiply.Text = "*";
this.btnMultiply.UseVisualStyleBackColor = true;
this.btnMultiply.Click += new System.EventHandler(this.btnMultiply_Click);
//
// btnDivide
//
this.btnDivide.Location = new System.Drawing.Point(80, 160);
this.btnDivide.Name = "btnDivide";
this.btnDivide.Size = new System.Drawing.Size(40, 40);
this.btnDivide.TabIndex = 5;
this.btnDivide.Text = "/";
this.btnDivide.UseVisualStyleBackColor = true;
this.btnDivide.Click += new System.EventHandler(this.btnDivide_Click);
//
// lblResult
//
this.lblResult.AutoSize = true;
this.lblResult.Location = new System.Drawing.Point(30, 220);
this.lblResult.Name = "lblResult";
this.lblResult.Size = new System.Drawing.Size(0, 13);
this.lblResult.TabIndex = 6;
//
// BasicCalculatorGUI
//
```

```csharp
        this.ClientSize = new System.Drawing.Size(200, 250);

        this.Controls.Add(this.lblResult);

        this.Controls.Add(this.btnDivide);

        this.Controls.Add(this.btnMultiply);

        this.Controls.Add(this.btnSubtract);

        this.Controls.Add(this.btnAdd);

        this.Controls.Add(this.txtNumber2);

        this.Controls.Add(this.txtNumber1);

        this.FormBorderStyle = System.Windows.Forms.FormBorderStyle.FixedSingle;

        this.MaximizeBox = false;

        this.Name = "BasicCalculatorGUI";

        this.Text = "Basic Calculator";

        this.ResumeLayout(false);

        this.PerformLayout();


    }


    private void btnAdd_Click(object sender, EventArgs e)

    {

        double num1 = double.Parse(txtNumber1.Text);

        double num2 = double.Parse(txtNumber2.Text);

        double result = num1 + num2;

        lblResult.Text = "Result: " + result;

    }


    private void btnSubtract_Click(object sender, EventArgs e)

    {

        double num1 = double.Parse(txtNumber1.Text);

        double num2 = double.Parse(txtNumber2.Text);

        double result = num1 - num2;

        lblResult.Text = "Result: " + result;
```

```csharp
    }

    private void btnMultiply_Click(object sender, EventArgs e)
    {
        double num1 = double.Parse(txtNumber1.Text);
        double num2 = double.Parse(txtNumber2.Text);
        double result = num1 * num2;
        lblResult.Text = "Result: " + result;
    }


    private void btnDivide_Click(object sender, EventArgs e)
    {
        double num1 = double.Parse(txtNumber1.Text);
        double num2 = double.Parse(txtNumber2.Text);
        if (num2 != 0)
        {
            double result = num1 / num2;
            lblResult.Text = "Result: " + result;
        }
        else
        {
            lblResult.Text = "Error: Division by zero.";
        }
    }
}
```

Digital Clock Program in C#

```csharp
using System;
using System.Windows.Forms;

class DigitalClock : Form
```

```csharp
{
    private Label lblTime;

    public DigitalClock()
    {
        InitializeComponent();
        Timer timer = new Timer();
        timer.Interval = 1000;
        timer.Tick += new EventHandler(timer_Tick);
        timer.Start();
    }

    private void InitializeComponent()
    {
        this.lblTime = new Label();
        this.SuspendLayout();
        //
        // lblTime
        //
        this.lblTime.AutoSize = true;
        this.lblTime.Font = new System.Drawing.Font("Arial", 24F,
System.Drawing.FontStyle.Regular, System.Drawing.GraphicsUnit.Point, ((byte)(0)));
        this.lblTime.Location = new System.Drawing.Point(20, 20);
        this.lblTime.Name = "lblTime";
        this.lblTime.Size = new System.Drawing.Size(0, 36);
        this.lblTime.TabIndex = 0;
        //
        // DigitalClock
        //
        this.ClientSize = new System.Drawing.Size(200, 100);
        this.Controls.Add(this.lblTime);
```

```csharp
        this.FormBorderStyle = System.Windows.Forms.FormBorderStyle.FixedSingle;

        this.MaximizeBox = false;

        this.Name = "DigitalClock";

        this.Text = "Digital Clock";

        this.ResumeLayout(false);

        this.PerformLayout();


    }


    private void timer_Tick(object sender, EventArgs e)

    {

        lblTime.Text = DateTime.Now.ToString("HH:mm:ss");

    }

}
```

Unit Converter Program in C#

```csharp
using System;

class UnitConverter

{

    static void Main()

    {

        Console.WriteLine("Unit Converter");

        Console.WriteLine("1. Length Converter");

        Console.WriteLine("2. Weight Converter");

        Console.Write("Enter your choice: ");

        int choice = Convert.ToInt32(Console.ReadLine());


        switch (choice)

        {

            case 1:

                LengthConverter();
```

```csharp
            break;
        case 2:
            WeightConverter();
            break;
        default:
            Console.WriteLine("Invalid choice.");
            break;
    }
}


static void LengthConverter()
{
    Console.WriteLine("Length Converter");
    Console.WriteLine("1. Feet to Meters");
    Console.WriteLine("2. Meters to Feet");
    Console.Write("Enter your choice: ");
    int choice = Convert.ToInt32(Console.ReadLine());

    switch (choice)
    {
        case 1:
            Console.Write("Enter length in feet: ");
            double feet = Convert.ToDouble(Console.ReadLine());
            double meters = feet * 0.3048;
            Console.WriteLine("Length in meters: " + meters);
            break;
        case 2:
            Console.Write("Enter length in meters: ");
            meters = Convert.ToDouble(Console.ReadLine());
            feet = meters / 0.3048;
            Console.WriteLine("Length in feet: " + feet);
```

```
            break;
        default:
            Console.WriteLine("Invalid choice.");
            break;
    }
}

static void WeightConverter()
{
    Console.WriteLine("Weight Converter");
    Console.WriteLine("1. Pounds to Kilograms");
    Console.WriteLine("2. Kilograms to Pounds");
    Console.Write("Enter your choice: ");
    int choice = Convert.ToInt32(Console.ReadLine());

    switch (choice)
    {
        case 1:
            Console.Write("Enter weight in pounds: ");
            double pounds = Convert.ToDouble(Console.ReadLine());
            double kilograms = pounds * 0.453592;
            Console.WriteLine("Weight in kilograms: " + kilograms);
            break;
        case 2:
            Console.Write("Enter weight in kilograms: ");
            kilograms = Convert.ToDouble(Console.ReadLine());
            pounds = kilograms / 0.453592;
            Console.WriteLine("Weight in pounds: " + pounds);
            break;
        default:
            Console.WriteLine("Invalid choice.");
```

```
        break;
    }
  }
}
```

Calendar Application Program in C#

```csharp
using System;

class CalendarApplication
{
  static void Main()
  {
    Console.WriteLine("Calendar Application");
    Console.WriteLine("1. Display Calendar");
    Console.WriteLine("2. Check Leap Year");
    Console.Write("Enter your choice: ");
    int choice = Convert.ToInt32(Console.ReadLine());

    switch (choice)
    {
      case 1:
        DisplayCalendar();
        break;
      case 2:
        CheckLeapYear();
        break;
      default:
        Console.WriteLine("Invalid choice.");
        break;
    }
  }

  static void DisplayCalendar()
  {
    Console.Write("Enter year: ");
    int year = Convert.ToInt32(Console.ReadLine());
```

```
    Console.Write("Enter month (1-12): ");
    int month = Convert.ToInt32(Console.ReadLine());

    DateTime date = new DateTime(year, month, 1);
    Console.WriteLine(date.ToString("MMMM yyyy"));
    Console.WriteLine("Sun Mon Tue Wed Thu Fri Sat");

    int daysInMonth = DateTime.DaysInMonth(year, month);
    int offset = (int)date.DayOfWeek;
    int day = 1;

    for (int i = 0; i < offset; i++)
    {
      Console.Write("    ");
    }

    for (int i = 0; i < daysInMonth; i++)
    {
      Console.Write(day.ToString().PadLeft(4));
      day++;

      if ((i + offset + 1) % 7 == 0 || i == daysInMonth - 1)
      {
        Console.WriteLine();
      }
    }
  }

static void CheckLeapYear()
{
```

```csharp
    Console.Write("Enter year: ");

    int year = Convert.ToInt32(Console.ReadLine());


    if (DateTime.IsLeapYear(year))

      Console.WriteLine(year + " is a leap year.");

    else

      Console.WriteLine(year + " is not a leap year.");

  }

}
```

Simple Paint Program Program in C#

```csharp
using System;

using System.Drawing;

using System.Windows.Forms;


class SimplePaintProgram : Form

{

  private Point startPoint = Point.Empty;

  private bool isDrawing = false;

  private Pen pen = new Pen(Color.Black, 2);


  public SimplePaintProgram()

  {

    this.DoubleBuffered = true;

    this.Paint += SimplePaintProgram_Paint;

    this.MouseDown += SimplePaintProgram_MouseDown;

    this.MouseMove += SimplePaintProgram_MouseMove;

    this.MouseUp += SimplePaintProgram_MouseUp;

  }


  private void SimplePaintProgram_Paint(object sender, PaintEventArgs e)
```

```csharp
    {
        e.Graphics.DrawLine(pen, startPoint, e.Location);
    }

    private void SimplePaintProgram_MouseDown(object sender, MouseEventArgs e)
    {
        isDrawing = true;
        startPoint = e.Location;
    }

    private void SimplePaintProgram_MouseMove(object sender, MouseEventArgs e)
    {
        if (isDrawing)
        {
            Invalidate();
        }
    }

    private void SimplePaintProgram_MouseUp(object sender, MouseEventArgs e)
    {
        isDrawing = false;
    }

    static void Main()
    {
        Application.Run(new SimplePaintProgram());
    }
}
```

Contact Management System Program in C#

```csharp
using System;
```

```csharp
using System.Collections.Generic;

class ContactManagementSystem
{
    static Dictionary<string, string> contacts = new Dictionary<string, string>();

    static void Main()
    {
        while (true)
        {
            Console.WriteLine("1. Add Contact");
            Console.WriteLine("2. View Contacts");
            Console.WriteLine("3. Search Contact");
            Console.WriteLine("4. Exit");
            Console.Write("Enter your choice: ");
            int choice = Convert.ToInt32(Console.ReadLine());

            switch (choice)
            {
                case 1:
                    AddContact();
                    break;
                case 2:
                    ViewContacts();
                    break;
                case 3:
                    SearchContact();
                    break;
                case 4:
                    return;
                default:
```

```csharp
            Console.WriteLine("Invalid choice. Please try again.");

            break;

        }

    }

}


    static void AddContact()

    {

        Console.Write("Enter contact name: ");

        string name = Console.ReadLine();

        Console.Write("Enter contact number: ");

        string number = Console.ReadLine();


        contacts[name] = number;

        Console.WriteLine("Contact added successfully.");

    }


    static void ViewContacts()

    {

        if (contacts.Count == 0)

        {

            Console.WriteLine("No contacts found.");

            return;

        }


        Console.WriteLine("Contacts:");

        foreach (KeyValuePair<string, string> contact in contacts)

        {

            Console.WriteLine(contact.Key + ": " + contact.Value);

        }

    }
```

```csharp
static void SearchContact()
  {
    Console.Write("Enter contact name to search: ");
    string name = Console.ReadLine();

    if (contacts.ContainsKey(name))
    {
      Console.WriteLine("Contact found:");
      Console.WriteLine(name + ": " + contacts[name]);
    }
    else
    {
      Console.WriteLine("Contact not found.");
    }
  }
}
```

Rock, Paper, Scissors Game Program in C#

```csharp
using System;
class RockPaperScissors
{
  static void Main()
  {
    while (true)
    {
      Console.WriteLine("Rock, Paper, Scissors Game");
      Console.WriteLine("1. Play Game");
      Console.WriteLine("2. Exit");
      Console.Write("Enter your choice: ");
      int choice = Convert.ToInt32(Console.ReadLine());
```

```csharp
        switch (choice)
        {
            case 1:
                PlayGame();
                break;
            case 2:
                return;
            default:
                Console.WriteLine("Invalid choice. Please try again.");
                break;
        }
    }
}

static void PlayGame()
{
    string[] choices = { "Rock", "Paper", "Scissors" };

    Console.WriteLine("Choose your move:");
    Console.WriteLine("1. Rock");
    Console.WriteLine("2. Paper");
    Console.WriteLine("3. Scissors");
    int playerChoice = Convert.ToInt32(Console.ReadLine()) - 1;
    Random random = new Random();
    int computerChoice = random.Next(0, 3);
    Console.WriteLine("Your move: " + choices[playerChoice]);
    Console.WriteLine("Computer's move: " + choices[computerChoice]);
    if (playerChoice == computerChoice)
    {
        Console.WriteLine("It's a tie!");
```

```csharp
        }
        else if ((playerChoice == 0 && computerChoice == 2) ||
            (playerChoice == 1 && computerChoice == 0) ||
            (playerChoice == 2 && computerChoice == 1))
        {
            Console.WriteLine("You win!");
        }
        else
        {
            Console.WriteLine("Computer wins!");
        }
    }
}
```

Basic Music Player Program in C#

```csharp
using System;
using System.Collections.Generic;
class BasicMusicPlayer
{
    static List<string> playlist = new List<string>();
    static int currentTrackIndex = -1;

    static void Main()
    {
        while (true)
        {
            Console.WriteLine("Basic Music Player");
            Console.WriteLine("1. Add Track to Playlist");
            Console.WriteLine("2. Play Next Track");
            Console.WriteLine("3. Play Previous Track");
```

```csharp
        Console.WriteLine("4. Show Playlist");

        Console.WriteLine("5. Exit");

        Console.Write("Enter your choice: ");

        int choice = Convert.ToInt32(Console.ReadLine());


        switch (choice)
        {
            case 1:
                AddTrack();
                break;
            case 2:
                PlayNextTrack();
                break;
            case 3:
                PlayPreviousTrack();
                break;
            case 4:
                ShowPlaylist();
                break;
            case 5:
                return;
            default:
                Console.WriteLine("Invalid choice. Please try again.");
                break;
        }
    }

    static void AddTrack()
    {
        Console.Write("Enter track name: ");
```

```csharp
        string trackName = Console.ReadLine();

        playlist.Add(trackName);

        Console.WriteLine("Track added to playlist.");

    }


    static void PlayNextTrack()

    {

        if (playlist.Count == 0)

        {

            Console.WriteLine("Playlist is empty.");

            return;

        }


        currentTrackIndex = (currentTrackIndex + 1) % playlist.Count;

        Console.WriteLine("Playing track: " + playlist[currentTrackIndex]);

    }


    static void PlayPreviousTrack()

    {

        if (playlist.Count == 0)

        {

            Console.WriteLine("Playlist is empty.");

            return;

        }


        currentTrackIndex = (currentTrackIndex - 1 + playlist.Count) % playlist.Count;

        Console.WriteLine("Playing track: " + playlist[currentTrackIndex]);

    }


    static void ShowPlaylist()

    {
```

```csharp
        Console.WriteLine("Playlist:");

        for (int i = 0; i < playlist.Count; i++)

        {

            Console.WriteLine((i + 1) + ". " + playlist[i]);

        }

    }

}


// Address Book Program in C#

using System;

using System.Collections.Generic;


class AddressBook

{

    static Dictionary<string, string> contacts = new Dictionary<string, string>();


    static void Main()

    {

        while (true)

        {

            Console.WriteLine("Address Book");

            Console.WriteLine("1. Add Contact");

            Console.WriteLine("2. View Contacts");

            Console.WriteLine("3. Search Contact");

            Console.WriteLine("4. Exit");

            Console.Write("Enter your choice: ");

            int choice = Convert.ToInt32(Console.ReadLine());


            switch (choice)

            {

                case 1:
```

```csharp
                AddContact();
                break;
            case 2:
                ViewContacts();
                break;
            case 3:
                SearchContact();
                break;
            case 4:
                return;
            default:
                Console.WriteLine("Invalid choice. Please try again.");
                break;
        }
    }
}

static void AddContact()
{
    Console.Write("Enter contact name: ");
    string name = Console.ReadLine();
    Console.Write("Enter contact number: ");
    string number = Console.ReadLine();

    contacts[name] = number;
    Console.WriteLine("Contact added successfully.");
}

static void ViewContacts()
{
    if (contacts.Count == 0)
```

```csharp
        {
            Console.WriteLine("No contacts found.");
            return;
        }

        Console.WriteLine("Contacts:");
        foreach (KeyValuePair<string, string> contact in contacts)
        {
            Console.WriteLine(contact.Key + ": " + contact.Value);
        }
    }

    static void SearchContact()
    {
        Console.Write("Enter contact name to search: ");
        string name = Console.ReadLine();

        if (contacts.ContainsKey(name))
        {
            Console.WriteLine("Contact found:");
            Console.WriteLine(name + ": " + contacts[name]);
        }
        else
        {
            Console.WriteLine("Contact not found.");
        }
    }
}
```

Simple Web Browser Program in C#

```csharp
using System;
```

```csharp
using System.Diagnostics;

class SimpleWebBrowser
{
    static void Main()
    {
        Console.Write("Enter URL: ");
        string url = Console.ReadLine();

        Process.Start(url);
    }
}
```

```csharp
// Image Viewer Program in C#

using System;
using System.Diagnostics;

class ImageViewer
{
    static void Main()
    {
        Console.Write("Enter image file path: ");
        string imagePath = Console.ReadLine();

        Process.Start(imagePath);
    }
}
```

Quiz Application Program in C#

Mastering Practical C-Sharp Programming

```csharp
using System;
using System.Collections.Generic;

class QuizApplication
{
    static Dictionary<string, string> questionsAndAnswers = new Dictionary<string, string>();

    static void Main()
    {
        Console.WriteLine("Quiz Application");
        LoadQuestionsAndAnswers();

        int score = 0;
        foreach (KeyValuePair<string, string> question in questionsAndAnswers)
        {
            Console.WriteLine(question.Key);
            string answer = Console.ReadLine();

            if (answer.ToLower() == question.Value.ToLower())
            {
                Console.WriteLine("Correct!");
                score++;
            }
            else
            {
                Console.WriteLine("Incorrect! Correct answer: " + question.Value);
            }
        }
```

```csharp
        Console.WriteLine("Quiz completed. Your score: " + score + "/" +
questionsAndAnswers.Count);
    }

    static void LoadQuestionsAndAnswers()
    {
        questionsAndAnswers.Add("What is the capital of France?", "Paris");
        questionsAndAnswers.Add("Who wrote 'Romeo and Juliet'?", "William
Shakespeare");
        questionsAndAnswers.Add("What is the chemical symbol for water?", "H2O");
        // Add more questions and answers as needed
    }
}
```

Snake Game Program in C#

```csharp
using System;
using System.Collections.Generic;
using System.Threading;

class SnakeGame
{
    static int width = 20;
    static int height = 10;
    static int snakeLength = 3;
    static int[] snakeX = new int[50];
    static int[] snakeY = new int[50];
    static int fruitX;
    static int fruitY;
    static bool gameOver;
    static Random random = new Random();
```

```csharp
    static void Main()
    {
        InitializeGame();
        while (!gameOver)
        {
            Draw();
            Input();
            Logic();
            Thread.Sleep(100);
        }
    }

    static void InitializeGame()
    {
        snakeX[0] = width / 2;
        snakeY[0] = height / 2;
        for (int i = 1; i < snakeLength; i++)
        {
            snakeX[i] = snakeX[i - 1] - 1;
            snakeY[i] = snakeY[i - 1];
        }
        GenerateFruit();
    }

    static void Draw()
    {
        Console.Clear();
        for (int i = 0; i < width + 2; i++)
            Console.Write("#");
        Console.WriteLine();
```

```csharp
    for (int i = 0; i < height; i++)
    {
        for (int j = 0; j < width; j++)
        {
            if (j == 0)
                Console.Write("#");
            if (i == snakeY[0] && j == snakeX[0])
                Console.Write("O");
            else if (i == fruitY && j == fruitX)
                Console.Write("F");
            else
            {
                bool print = false;
                for (int k = 1; k < snakeLength; k++)
                {
                    if (snakeY[k] == i && snakeX[k] == j)
                    {
                        Console.Write("o");
                        print = true;
                    }
                }
                if (!print)
                    Console.Write(" ");
            }
            if (j == width - 1)
                Console.Write("#");
        }
        Console.WriteLine();
    }

    for (int i = 0; i < width + 2; i++)
```

```csharp
        Console.Write("#");

    Console.WriteLine();

    Console.WriteLine("Score: " + (snakeLength - 3));
}


static void Input()
{
    if (Console.KeyAvailable)
    {
        ConsoleKeyInfo key = Console.ReadKey(true);
        switch (key.Key)
        {
            case ConsoleKey.UpArrow:
                if (snakeLength == 1 || snakeY[0] != snakeY[1] + 1)
                {
                    snakeY[0]--;
                }
                break;
            case ConsoleKey.DownArrow:
                if (snakeLength == 1 || snakeY[0] != snakeY[1] - 1)
                {
                    snakeY[0]++;
                }
                break;
            case ConsoleKey.LeftArrow:
                if (snakeLength == 1 || snakeX[0] != snakeX[1] + 1)
                {
                    snakeX[0]--;
                }
                break;
            case ConsoleKey.RightArrow:
```

```csharp
            if (snakeLength == 1 || snakeX[0] != snakeX[1] - 1)

                {

                    snakeX[0]++;

                }

                break;

            }

        }

    }

    static void Logic()

    {

        if (snakeX[0] == fruitX && snakeY[0] == fruitY)

        {

            GenerateFruit();

            snakeLength++;

        }

        if (snakeX[0] == width || snakeX[0] == -1 || snakeY[0] == height || snakeY[0] == -
1)

        {

            gameOver = true;

            return;

        }

        for (int i = 1; i < snakeLength; i++)

        {

            if (snakeX[0] == snakeX[i] && snakeY[0] == snakeY[i])

            {

                gameOver = true;

                return;

            }

        }

        for (int i = snakeLength - 1; i > 0; i--)
```

```
        {
            snakeX[i] = snakeX[i - 1];
            snakeY[i] = snakeY[i - 1];
        }
    }


    static void GenerateFruit()
    {
        fruitX = random.Next(0, width);
        fruitY = random.Next(0, height);
    }
}
```

Chat Application Program in C#

```
using System;
using System.Net;
using System.Net.Sockets;
using System.Text;
using System.Threading;

class ChatApplication
{
    static readonly IPAddress ipAddress = IPAddress.Parse("127.0.0.1");
    static readonly int port = 8888;
    static TcpListener server = new TcpListener(ipAddress, port);
    static TcpClient client;
    static NetworkStream stream;

    static void Main()
    {
        Console.WriteLine("Chat Application");
```

```csharp
        Console.Write("Enter your username: ");
        string username = Console.ReadLine();

        Console.WriteLine("Waiting for connection...");
        server.Start();
        client = server.AcceptTcpClient();
        stream = client.GetStream();

        Thread receiveThread = new Thread(ReceiveMessage);
        receiveThread.Start();

        while (true)
        {
            string message = Console.ReadLine();
            SendMessage(username + ": " + message);
        }
    }

    static void ReceiveMessage()
    {
        while (true)
        {
            byte[] buffer = new byte[256];
            StringBuilder message = new StringBuilder();
            int bytes = 0;

            do
            {
                bytes = stream.Read(buffer, 0, buffer.Length);
                message.Append(Encoding.Unicode.GetString(buffer, 0, bytes));
```

```csharp
        } while (stream.DataAvailable);

        Console.WriteLine(message);
    }
}

    static void SendMessage(string message)
    {
        byte[] data = Encoding.Unicode.GetBytes(message);
        stream.Write(data, 0, data.Length);
    }
}
```

Blackjack Game Program in C#

```csharp
using System;
using System.Collections.Generic;

class BlackjackGame
{
    static Random random = new Random();
    static Dictionary<string, int> deck = new Dictionary<string, int>()
    {
        {"2", 2}, {"3", 3}, {"4", 4}, {"5", 5}, {"6", 6}, {"7", 7}, {"8", 8}, {"9", 9}, {"10",
10},
        {"Jack", 10}, {"Queen", 10}, {"King", 10}, {"Ace", 11}
    };

    static void Main()
    {
        Console.WriteLine("Blackjack Game");
        int playerScore = 0;
```

```csharp
    int dealerScore = 0;

    DealCard("Player", ref playerScore);
    DealCard("Dealer", ref dealerScore);
    DealCard("Player", ref playerScore);
    DealCard("Dealer", ref dealerScore, true);

    while (playerScore < 21)
    {
        Console.Write("Do you want to hit (h) or stand (s)? ");
        char choice = Console.ReadKey().KeyChar;
        Console.WriteLine();

        if (choice == 'h')
        {
            DealCard("Player", ref playerScore);
        }
        else if (choice == 's')
        {
            break;
        }
        else
        {
            Console.WriteLine("Invalid choice. Please try again.");
        }
    }

    if (playerScore > 21)
    {
        Console.WriteLine("Player busts! Dealer wins.");
        return;
```

```csharp
    }

    while (dealerScore < 17)
    {
        DealCard("Dealer", ref dealerScore);
    }

    if (dealerScore > 21 || playerScore > dealerScore)
    {
        Console.WriteLine("Player wins!");
    }
    else if (dealerScore > playerScore)
    {
        Console.WriteLine("Dealer wins.");
    }
    else
    {
        Console.WriteLine("It's a tie!");
    }
}

static void DealCard(string player, ref int score, bool showCard = false)
{
    string card = GetRandomCard();
    int cardValue = deck[card];
    if (player == "Dealer" && !showCard)
    {
        Console.WriteLine("Dealer deals a card face down.");
    }
    else
    {
```

```csharp
        Console.WriteLine(player + " receives a " + card + ".");

        score += cardValue;

        Console.WriteLine(player + "'s current score: " + score);

      }

  }


  static string GetRandomCard()

  {

    List<string> cards = new List<string>(deck.Keys);

    int index = random.Next(cards.Count);

    return cards[index];

  }

}
```

Hangman Game Program in C#

```csharp
using System;

class HangmanGame

{

  static string[] words = { "apple", "banana", "orange", "grape", "melon" };

  static Random random = new Random();

  static string wordToGuess;

  static char[] guessedWord;

  static int attemptsLeft = 6;


  static void Main()

  {

    Console.WriteLine("Hangman Game");


    wordToGuess = words[random.Next(words.Length)];

    guessedWord = new char[wordToGuess.Length];
```

```csharp
    for (int i = 0; i < guessedWord.Length; i++)
    {
      guessedWord[i] = '_';
    }

    while (attemptsLeft > 0)
    {
      Console.WriteLine("Attempts left: " + attemptsLeft);
      Console.WriteLine("Guessed word: " + new string(guessedWord));

      Console.Write("Enter a letter: ");
      char letter = Console.ReadLine()[0];

      if (!GuessLetter(letter))
      {
        attemptsLeft--;
      }

      if (string.Equals(wordToGuess, new string(guessedWord)))
      {
        Console.WriteLine("Congratulations! You guessed the word: " +
wordToGuess);
        return;
      }
    }

    Console.WriteLine("Sorry, you're out of attempts. The word was: " +
wordToGuess);
  }

  static bool GuessLetter(char letter)
```

```
    {
        bool correctGuess = false;
        for (int i = 0; i < wordToGuess.Length; i++)
        {
            if (wordToGuess[i] == letter)
            {
                guessedWord[i] = letter;
                correctGuess = true;
            }
        }
        return correctGuess;
    }
}
```

Memory Game Program in C#

```
using System;
using System.Collections.Generic;
class MemoryGame
{
    static char[,] board = new char[4, 4];
    static List<char> symbols = new List<char>() { 'A', 'B', 'C', 'D', 'E', 'F', 'G', 'H' };
    static Random random = new Random();

    static void Main()
    {
        InitializeBoard();
        ShuffleSymbols();

        while (!GameIsOver())
        {
            DisplayBoard();
```

```csharp
        int[] firstCard = SelectCard();

      int[] secondCard = SelectCard();


      if (firstCard[0] == secondCard[0] && firstCard[1] == secondCard[1])

      {

        Console.WriteLine("You selected the same card twice. Try again.");

        continue;

      }


      if (board[firstCard[0], firstCard[1]] != ' ' || board[secondCard[0], secondCard[1]]
!= ' ')

      {

      Console.WriteLine("One or both of the selected cards have already been
matched. Try again.");

        continue;

      }


      if (symbols[firstCard[2]] == symbols[secondCard[2]])

      {

        board[firstCard[0], firstCard[1]] = symbols[firstCard[2]];

        board[secondCard[0], secondCard[1]] = symbols[secondCard[2]];

        Console.WriteLine("Match found!");

      }

      else

      {

        Console.WriteLine("No match. Try again.");

      }

    }


    Console.WriteLine("Congratulations! You've matched all the cards.");

  }
```

```csharp
static void InitializeBoard()
{
    for (int i = 0; i < 4; i++)
    {
        for (int j = 0; j < 4; j++)
        {
            board[i, j] = ' ';
        }
    }
}

static void ShuffleSymbols()
{
    for (int i = 0; i < symbols.Count; i++)
    {
        int randomIndex = random.Next(i, symbols.Count);
        char temp = symbols[i];
        symbols[i] = symbols[randomIndex];
        symbols[randomIndex] = temp;
    }
}

static void DisplayBoard()
{
    Console.WriteLine("  1 2 3 4");
    for (int i = 0; i < 4; i++)
    {
        Console.Write(i + 1 + " ");
        for (int j = 0; j < 4; j++)
        {
            {
```

```csharp
            Console.Write(board[i, j] + " ");
        }
        Console.WriteLine();
    }
}

static int[] SelectCard()
{
    int[] card = new int[3];
    Console.Write("Enter row number (1-4): ");
    card[0] = Convert.ToInt32(Console.ReadLine()) - 1;
    Console.Write("Enter column number (1-4): ");
    card[1] = Convert.ToInt32(Console.ReadLine()) - 1;
    card[2] = card[0] * 4 + card[1];
    return card;
}

static bool GameIsOver()
{
    foreach (char symbol in symbols)
    {
        bool symbolFound = false;
        for (int i = 0; i < 4; i++)
        {
            for (int j = 0; j < 4; j++)
            {
                if (board[i, j] == symbol)
                {
                    symbolFound = true;
                    break;
                }
```

```
            }

         if (symbolFound) break;

      }

      if (!symbolFound) return false;

   }

   return true;

 }

}


```

Sudoku Solver Program in C#

```
using System;

class SudokuSolver

{

   static int[,] board = new int[9, 9];

   static void Main()

   {

     InitializeBoard();

     if (SolveSudoku())

     {

        Console.WriteLine("Sudoku puzzle solved:");

        PrintBoard();

     }

     else

     {

        Console.WriteLine("No solution exists for the given Sudoku puzzle.");

     }

   }

   static void InitializeBoard()
```

```csharp
    {
        // Initialize the board with the Sudoku puzzle
        // 0 represents empty cells
    }

    static bool SolveSudoku()
    {
        int row = -1;
        int col = -1;
        bool isEmpty = true;

        for (int i = 0; i < 9; i++)
        {
            for (int j = 0; j < 9; j++)
            {
                if (board[i, j] == 0)
                {
                    row = i;
                    col = j;
                    isEmpty = false;
                    break;
                }
            }
            if (!isEmpty)
            {
                break;
            }
        }

        if (isEmpty)
        {
```

```csharp
        return true;
    }

    for (int num = 1; num <= 9; num++)
    {
        if (IsSafe(row, col, num))
        {
            board[row, col] = num;
            if (SolveSudoku())
            {
                return true;
            }
            else
            {
                board[row, col] = 0;
            }
        }
    }

    return false;
}


static bool IsSafe(int row, int col, int num)
{
    return !UsedInRow(row, num) && !UsedInColumn(col, num) &&
!UsedInBox(row - row % 3, col - col % 3, num);
}


static bool UsedInRow(int row, int num)
{
    for (int i = 0; i < 9; i++)
```

```csharp
    {
        if (board[row, i] == num)
        {
            return true;
        }
    }
    return false;
}

static bool UsedInColumn(int col, int num)
{
    for (int i = 0; i < 9; i++)
    {
        if (board[i, col] == num)
        {
            return true;
        }
    }
    return false;
}

static bool UsedInBox(int boxStartRow, int boxStartCol, int num)
{
    for (int i = 0; i < 3; i++)
    {
        for (int j = 0; j < 3; j++)
        {
            if (board[i + boxStartRow, j + boxStartCol] == num)
            {
                return true;
            }
```

```csharp
        }

    }

    return false;

}


static void PrintBoard()

{

    for (int i = 0; i < 9; i++)

    {

        for (int j = 0; j < 9; j++)

        {

            Console.Write(board[i, j] + " ");

        }

        Console.WriteLine();

    }

}

}
```

Basic Drawing Program Program in C#

```csharp
using System;

using System.Drawing;

using System.Windows.Forms;


class BasicDrawingProgram : Form

{

    private Point startPoint = Point.Empty;

    private bool isDrawing = false;

    private Pen pen = new Pen(Color.Black, 2);


    public BasicDrawingProgram()

    {
```

```csharp
        this.DoubleBuffered = true;

        this.Paint += BasicDrawingProgram_Paint;

        this.MouseDown += BasicDrawingProgram_MouseDown;

        this.MouseMove += BasicDrawingProgram_MouseMove;

        this.MouseUp += BasicDrawingProgram_MouseUp;

    }


    private void BasicDrawingProgram_Paint(object sender, PaintEventArgs e)

    {

        if (isDrawing)

        {

            e.Graphics.DrawLine(pen, startPoint, PointToClient(Cursor.Position));

        }

    }


    private void BasicDrawingProgram_MouseDown(object sender, MouseEventArgs e)

    {

        startPoint = e.Location;

        isDrawing = true;

    }


    private void BasicDrawingProgram_MouseMove(object sender, MouseEventArgs e)

    {

        if (isDrawing)

        {

            Invalidate();

        }

    }

    private void BasicDrawingProgram_MouseUp(object sender, MouseEventArgs e)

    {
```

```csharp
        isDrawing = false;
    }


    static void Main()
    {
        Application.Run(new BasicDrawingProgram());
    }
}
```

Barcode Scanner Program in C#

```csharp
using System;
class BarcodeScanner
{
    static void Main()
    {
        Console.WriteLine("Barcode Scanner");
        Console.Write("Enter barcode: ");
        string barcode = Console.ReadLine();
        if (IsValidBarcode(barcode))
        {
            Console.WriteLine("Valid barcode.");
        }
        else
        {
            Console.WriteLine("Invalid barcode.");
        }
    }

    static bool IsValidBarcode(string barcode)
    {
        // Logic to validate the barcode
```

```csharp
        return barcode.Length == 10;

    }

}
```

Expense Tracker Program in C#

```csharp
using System;

using System.Collections.Generic;


class ExpenseTracker

{

    static Dictionary<string, double> expenses = new Dictionary<string, double>();


    static void Main()

    {

        while (true)

        {

            Console.WriteLine("Expense Tracker");

            Console.WriteLine("1. Add Expense");

            Console.WriteLine("2. View Expenses");

            Console.WriteLine("3. Exit");

            Console.Write("Enter your choice: ");

            int choice = Convert.ToInt32(Console.ReadLine());


            switch (choice)

            {

                case 1:

                    AddExpense();

                    break;

                case 2:

                    ViewExpenses();

                    break;
```

```csharp
            case 3:
                return;
            default:
                Console.WriteLine("Invalid choice. Please try again.");
                break;
        }
    }
}

static void AddExpense()
{
    Console.Write("Enter expense description: ");
    string description = Console.ReadLine();
    Console.Write("Enter expense amount: ");
    double amount = Convert.ToDouble(Console.ReadLine());

    expenses[description] = amount;
    Console.WriteLine("Expense added successfully.");
}

static void ViewExpenses()
{
    if (expenses.Count == 0)
    {
        Console.WriteLine("No expenses found.");
        return;
    }

    Console.WriteLine("Expenses:");
    foreach (KeyValuePair<string, double> expense in expenses)
    {
```

```
        Console.WriteLine(expense.Key + ": $" + expense.Value);

    }

  }

}


// Weather Application Program in C#
using System;

class WeatherApplication
{
  static void Main()
  {
    Console.WriteLine("Weather Application");
    Console.Write("Enter your location: ");
    string location = Console.ReadLine();

    // Logic to fetch weather information for the specified location
    Console.WriteLine("Weather information for " + location + ": Sunny, 25°C");
  }
}


// Note-taking App Program in C#
using System;
using System.Collections.Generic;

class NoteTakingApp
{
  static List<string> notes = new List<string>();

  static void Main()
  {
```

```csharp
        while (true)
    {
        Console.WriteLine("Note-taking App");
        Console.WriteLine("1. Add Note");
        Console.WriteLine("2. View Notes");
        Console.WriteLine("3. Exit");
        Console.Write("Enter your choice: ");
        int choice = Convert.ToInt32(Console.ReadLine());

        switch (choice)
        {
            case 1:
                AddNote();
                break;
            case 2:
                ViewNotes();
                break;
            case 3:
                return;
            default:
                Console.WriteLine("Invalid choice. Please try again.");
                break;
        }
    }
}

static void AddNote()
{
    Console.Write("Enter your note: ");
    string note = Console.ReadLine();
    notes.Add(note);
```

```csharp
      Console.WriteLine("Note added successfully.");

  }

  static void ViewNotes()
  {
    if (notes.Count == 0)
    {
      Console.WriteLine("No notes found.");
      return;
    }

    Console.WriteLine("Notes:");
    for (int i = 0; i < notes.Count; i++)
    {
      Console.WriteLine((i + 1) + ". " + notes[i]);
    }
  }
}


// Task Scheduler Program in C#
using System;
using System.Collections.Generic;

class TaskScheduler
{
  static Dictionary<DateTime, string> tasks = new Dictionary<DateTime, string>();

  static void Main()
  {
    while (true)
    {
```

```csharp
        Console.WriteLine("Task Scheduler");

        Console.WriteLine("1. Add Task");

        Console.WriteLine("2. View Tasks");

        Console.WriteLine("3. Exit");

        Console.Write("Enter your choice: ");

        int choice = Convert.ToInt32(Console.ReadLine());


        switch (choice)

        {

          case 1:

            AddTask();

            break;

          case 2:

            ViewTasks();

            break;

          case 3:

            return;

          default:

            Console.WriteLine("Invalid choice. Please try again.");

            break;

        }

      }

    }


  static void AddTask()

  {

    Console.Write("Enter task description: ");

    string description = Console.ReadLine();

    Console.Write("Enter task due date (MM/dd/yyyy HH:mm): ");

    DateTime dueDate = DateTime.ParseExact(Console.ReadLine(), "MM/dd/yyyy
HH:mm", null);
```

```csharp
      tasks[dueDate] = description;
      Console.WriteLine("Task added successfully.");
    }


    static void ViewTasks()
    {
      if (tasks.Count == 0)
      {
        Console.WriteLine("No tasks found.");
        return;
      }


      Console.WriteLine("Tasks:");
      foreach (KeyValuePair<DateTime, string> task in tasks)
      {
        Console.WriteLine(task.Key.ToString("MM/dd/yyyy HH:mm") + ": " +
task.Value);
      }
    }
}


// Countdown Timer Program in C#
using System;
using System.Threading;


class CountdownTimer
{
  static void Main()
  {
    Console.WriteLine("Countdown Timer");
```

```csharp
        Console.Write("Enter countdown time (in seconds): ");

        int seconds = Convert.ToInt32(Console.ReadLine());


        Console.WriteLine("Countdown started...");

        for (int i = seconds; i >= 0; i--)

        {

            Console.WriteLine("Time remaining: " + i + " seconds");

            Thread.Sleep(1000);

        }


        Console.WriteLine("Time's up!");

    }

}
```

Chess Game Program in C#

```csharp
// Chess Game Program in C#

using System;

class ChessGame
{
    static void Main()
    {
        Console.WriteLine("Chess Game");

        // Initialize chess board
        char[,] chessBoard = InitializeChessBoard();

        // Display initial chess board
        DisplayChessBoard(chessBoard);
```

```csharp
        // Logic to play the chess game
    }

    static char[,] InitializeChessBoard()
    {
        char[,] board = new char[8, 8]
        {
            {'R', 'N', 'B', 'Q', 'K', 'B', 'N', 'R'},
            {'P', 'P', 'P', 'P', 'P', 'P', 'P', 'P'},
            {' ', ' ', ' ', ' ', ' ', ' ', ' ', ' '},
            {' ', ' ', ' ', ' ', ' ', ' ', ' ', ' '},
            {' ', ' ', ' ', ' ', ' ', ' ', ' ', ' '},
            {' ', ' ', ' ', ' ', ' ', ' ', ' ', ' '},
            {'p', 'p', 'p', 'p', 'p', 'p', 'p', 'p'},
            {'r', 'n', 'b', 'q', 'k', 'b', 'n', 'r'}
        };

        return board;
    }

    static void DisplayChessBoard(char[,] board)
    {
        Console.WriteLine("  a b c d e f g h");
        Console.WriteLine("  ----------------");
        for (int i = 0; i < 8; i++)
        {
            Console.Write(8 - i + "|");
            for (int j = 0; j < 8; j++)
            {
                Console.Write(board[i, j] + " ");
            }
```

```
        Console.WriteLine("|" + (8 - i));
    }

    Console.WriteLine("  ----------------");
    Console.WriteLine("  a b c d e f g h");
  }
}
```

Binary Converter Program in C#

```
using System;

class BinaryConverter
{
  static void Main()
  {
    Console.WriteLine("Binary Converter");
    Console.Write("Enter a binary number: ");
    string binaryNumber = Console.ReadLine();

    // Logic to convert binary number to decimal
    int decimalNumber = Convert.ToInt32(binaryNumber, 2);
    Console.WriteLine("Decimal equivalent: " + decimalNumber);
  }
}

// Morse Code Translator Program in C#

using System;
using System.Collections.Generic;

class MorseCodeTranslator
{
```

```csharp
    static Dictionary<char, string> morseCodeMap = new Dictionary<char, string>()
    {
        {'A', ".-"}, {'B', "-..."}, {'C', "-.-."}, {'D', "-.."}, {'E', "."},
        {'F', "..-."}, {'G', "--."}, {'H', "...."}, {'I', ".."}, {'J', ".---"},
        {'K', "-.-"}, {'L', ".-.."}, {'M', "--"}, {'N', "-."}, {'O', "---"},
        {'P', ".--."}, {'Q', "--.-"}, {'R', ".-."}, {'S', "..."}, {'T', "-"},
        {'U', "..-"}, {'V', "...-"}, {'W', ".--"}, {'X', "-..-"}, {'Y', "-.--"},
        {'Z', "--.."}, {'1', ".----"}, {'2', "..---"}, {'3', "...--"}, {'4', "....-"},
        {'5', "....."}, {'6', "-...."}, {'7', "--..."}, {'8', "---.."}, {'9', "----."},
        {'0', "-----"}, {' ', " "}
    };

    static void Main()
    {
        Console.WriteLine("Morse Code Translator");
        Console.WriteLine("1. Text to Morse Code");
        Console.WriteLine("2. Morse Code to Text");
        Console.Write("Enter your choice: ");
        int choice = Convert.ToInt32(Console.ReadLine());

        switch (choice)
        {
            case 1:
                TextToMorseCode();
                break;
            case 2:
                MorseCodeToText();
                break;
            default:
                Console.WriteLine("Invalid choice. Please try again.");
                break;
```

```csharp
        }

    }


    static void TextToMorseCode()
    {
        Console.Write("Enter text to convert to Morse code: ");
        string text = Console.ReadLine().ToUpper();

        string morseCode = "";
        foreach (char c in text)
        {
            if (morseCodeMap.ContainsKey(c))
            {
                morseCode += morseCodeMap[c] + " ";
            }
        }

        Console.WriteLine("Morse code: " + morseCode);
    }

    static void MorseCodeToText()
    {
        Console.Write("Enter Morse code to convert to text: ");
        string morseCode = Console.ReadLine();

        string[] morseCodeWords = morseCode.Split(new char[] { ' ' },
StringSplitOptions.RemoveEmptyEntries);
        string text = "";
        foreach (string morseWord in morseCodeWords)
        {
            foreach (KeyValuePair<char, string> kvp in morseCodeMap)
```

```
        {
            if (kvp.Value == morseWord)
            {
                text += kvp.Key;
                break;
            }
          }
        }


      Console.WriteLine("Text: " + text);
    }
}
```

Budget Planner Program in C#

```
using System;
using System.Collections.Generic;

class BudgetPlanner
{
    static Dictionary<string, double> expenses = new Dictionary<string, double>();

    static void Main()
    {
        while (true)
        {
            Console.WriteLine("Budget Planner");
            Console.WriteLine("1. Add Expense");
            Console.WriteLine("2. View Expenses");
            Console.WriteLine("3. Exit");
            Console.Write("Enter your choice: ");
            int choice = Convert.ToInt32(Console.ReadLine());
```

```csharp
        switch (choice)
        {
            case 1:
                AddExpense();
                break;
            case 2:
                ViewExpenses();
                break;
            case 3:
                return;
            default:
                Console.WriteLine("Invalid choice. Please try again.");
                break;
        }
    }
}

static void AddExpense()
{
    Console.Write("Enter expense description: ");
    string description = Console.ReadLine();
    Console.Write("Enter expense amount: ");
    double amount = Convert.ToDouble(Console.ReadLine());

    expenses[description] = amount;
    Console.WriteLine("Expense added successfully.");
}

static void ViewExpenses()
{
```

```csharp
        if (expenses.Count == 0)

        {

            Console.WriteLine("No expenses found.");

            return;

        }


        Console.WriteLine("Expenses:");

        foreach (KeyValuePair<string, double> expense in expenses)

        {

            Console.WriteLine(expense.Key + ": $" + expense.Value);

        }

    }

}
```

Word Counter Program in C#

```csharp
using System;

class WordCounter

{

    static void Main()

    {

        Console.WriteLine("Word Counter");

        Console.Write("Enter a sentence: ");

        string sentence = Console.ReadLine();


        int wordCount = CountWords(sentence);

        Console.WriteLine("Number of words: " + wordCount);

    }


    static int CountWords(string sentence)

    {
```

```csharp
    string[] words = sentence.Split(new char[] { ' ' },
StringSplitOptions.RemoveEmptyEntries);
    return words.Length;
  }
}
```

Image Slider Program in C#

```csharp
using System;
using System.IO;
using System.Threading;

class ImageSlider
{
  static void Main()
  {
    Console.WriteLine("Image Slider");
    Console.Write("Enter folder path containing images: ");
    string folderPath = Console.ReadLine();

    string[] imageFiles = Directory.GetFiles(folderPath, "*.jpg");
    if (imageFiles.Length == 0)
    {
      Console.WriteLine("No JPG images found in the specified folder.");
      return;
    }

    while (true)
    {
      foreach (string imagePath in imageFiles)
      {
        Console.Clear();
```

```csharp
            Console.WriteLine("Current Image: " + Path.GetFileName(imagePath));

        // Display the image or image path as needed

        Thread.Sleep(2000); // 2 seconds delay between images

      }

    }

  }

}
```

File Compressor/Decompressor Program in C#

```csharp
using System;

using System.IO;

using System.IO.Compression;


class FileCompressorDecompressor

{

  static void Main()

  {

    Console.WriteLine("File Compressor/Decompressor");

    Console.WriteLine("1. Compress File");

    Console.WriteLine("2. Decompress File");

    Console.Write("Enter your choice: ");

    int choice = Convert.ToInt32(Console.ReadLine());


    switch (choice)

    {

      case 1:

        CompressFile();

        break;

      case 2:

        DecompressFile();

        break;
```

```
        default:
            Console.WriteLine("Invalid choice. Please try again.");
            break;
    }
}


  static void CompressFile()
  {
    Console.Write("Enter file path to compress: ");
    string filePath = Console.ReadLine();
    string compressedFilePath = filePath + ".gz";
    using (FileStream originalFileStream = File.OpenRead(filePath))
    {
      using (FileStream compressedFileStream = File.Create(compressedFilePath))
      {
        using (GZipStream compressionStream = new
GZipStream(compressedFileStream, CompressionMode.Compress))
        {
            originalFileStream.CopyTo(compressionStream);
        }
      }
    }


    Console.WriteLine("File compressed successfully. Compressed file saved as: " +
compressedFilePath);
  }

  static void DecompressFile()
  {
    Console.Write("Enter compressed file path to decompress: ");
    string compressedFilePath = Console.ReadLine();
```

```csharp
    string decompressedFilePath = compressedFilePath.Replace(".gz", "");

    using (FileStream originalFileStream = File.OpenRead(compressedFilePath))
    {
      using (FileStream decompressedFileStream =
File.Create(decompressedFilePath))
      {
        using (GZipStream decompressionStream = new
GZipStream(originalFileStream, CompressionMode.Decompress))
        {
          decompressionStream.CopyTo(decompressedFileStream);
        }
      }
    }

    Console.WriteLine("File decompressed successfully. Decompressed file saved as: "
+ decompressedFilePath);
  }
}
```

Recipe Manager Program in C#

```csharp
using System;
using System.Collections.Generic;

class RecipeManager
{
    static Dictionary<string, string> recipes = new Dictionary<string, string>();

    static void Main()
    {
      while (true)
```

```csharp
    {
        Console.WriteLine("Recipe Manager");
        Console.WriteLine("1. Add Recipe");
        Console.WriteLine("2. View Recipe");
        Console.WriteLine("3. Exit");
        Console.Write("Enter your choice: ");
        int choice = Convert.ToInt32(Console.ReadLine());

        switch (choice)
        {
            case 1:
                AddRecipe();
                break;
            case 2:
                ViewRecipe();
                break;
            case 3:
                return;
            default:
                Console.WriteLine("Invalid choice. Please try again.");
                break;
        }
    }
}

static void AddRecipe()
{
    Console.Write("Enter recipe name: ");
    string recipeName = Console.ReadLine();
    Console.Write("Enter recipe details: ");
    string recipeDetails = Console.ReadLine();
```

```csharp
      recipes[recipeName] = recipeDetails;
      Console.WriteLine("Recipe added successfully.");
   }

   static void ViewRecipe()
   {
     if (recipes.Count == 0)
     {
       Console.WriteLine("No recipes found.");
        return;
     }

     Console.WriteLine("Recipes:");
     foreach (KeyValuePair<string, string> recipe in recipes)
     {
       Console.WriteLine("Name: " + recipe.Key);
       Console.WriteLine("Details: " + recipe.Value);
       Console.WriteLine();
     }
   }
}
```

Movie Database Program in C#

```csharp
using System;
using System.Collections.Generic;

class MovieDatabase
{
   static Dictionary<string, string> movies = new Dictionary<string, string>();
```

```csharp
    static void Main()
  {
    while (true)
    {
      Console.WriteLine("Movie Database");
      Console.WriteLine("1. Add Movie");
      Console.WriteLine("2. View Movies");
      Console.WriteLine("3. Exit");
      Console.Write("Enter your choice: ");
      int choice = Convert.ToInt32(Console.ReadLine());

      switch (choice)
      {
        case 1:
          AddMovie();
          break;
        case 2:
          ViewMovies();
          break;
        case 3:
          return;
        default:
          Console.WriteLine("Invalid choice. Please try again.");
          break;
      }
    }
  }

  static void AddMovie()
  {
    Console.Write("Enter movie title: ");
```

```csharp
        string movieTitle = Console.ReadLine();

        Console.Write("Enter movie details: ");

        string movieDetails = Console.ReadLine();


        movies[movieTitle] = movieDetails;

        Console.WriteLine("Movie added successfully.");

    }


    static void ViewMovies()

    {

      if (movies.Count == 0)

      {

        Console.WriteLine("No movies found.");

        return;

      }


      Console.WriteLine("Movies:");

      foreach (KeyValuePair<string, string> movie in movies)

      {

        Console.WriteLine("Title: " + movie.Key);

        Console.WriteLine("Details: " + movie.Value);

        Console.WriteLine();

      }

    }

}
```

Student Grade Tracker Program in C#

```csharp
using System;

using System.Collections.Generic;


class StudentGradeTracker
```

```csharp
{
    static Dictionary<string, List<int>> studentGrades = new Dictionary<string,
List<int>>();

    static void Main()
    {
        while (true)
        {
            Console.WriteLine("Student Grade Tracker");
            Console.WriteLine("1. Add Student Grades");
            Console.WriteLine("2. View Student Grades");
            Console.WriteLine("3. Exit");
            Console.Write("Enter your choice: ");
            int choice = Convert.ToInt32(Console.ReadLine());

            switch (choice)
            {
                case 1:
                    AddStudentGrades();
                    break;
                case 2:
                    ViewStudentGrades();
                    break;
                case 3:
                    return;
                default:
                    Console.WriteLine("Invalid choice. Please try again.");
                    break;
            }
        }
    }
```

```csharp
static void AddStudentGrades()
{
    Console.Write("Enter student name: ");
    string studentName = Console.ReadLine();
    Console.Write("Enter comma-separated grades: ");
    string gradesInput = Console.ReadLine();
    string[] gradesArray = gradesInput.Split(',');
    List<int> grades = new List<int>();

    foreach (string gradeStr in gradesArray)
    {
        int grade;
        if (int.TryParse(gradeStr.Trim(), out grade))
        {
            grades.Add(grade);
        }
        else
        {
            Console.WriteLine("Invalid grade format. Skipping...");
        }
    }

    studentGrades[studentName] = grades;
    Console.WriteLine("Grades added successfully for " + studentName);
}

static void ViewStudentGrades()
{
    if (studentGrades.Count == 0)
    {
```

```
        Console.WriteLine("No student grades found.");

        return;

    }


    Console.WriteLine("Student Grades:");

    foreach (KeyValuePair<string, List<int>> student in studentGrades)

    {

        Console.WriteLine("Student Name: " + student.Key);

        Console.WriteLine("Grades: " + string.Join(", ", student.Value));

        Console.WriteLine();

    }

  }

}
```

Password Generator Program in C#

```
using System;

class PasswordGenerator

{

  static void Main()

  {

    Console.WriteLine("Password Generator");

    Console.Write("Enter password length: ");

    int passwordLength = Convert.ToInt32(Console.ReadLine());


    string password = GeneratePassword(passwordLength);

    Console.WriteLine("Generated Password: " + password);

  }


  static string GeneratePassword(int length)

  {
```

Mastering Practical C-Sharp Programming

```csharp
        const string validChars =
"abcdefghijklmnopqrstuvwxyzABCDEFGHIJKLMNOPQRSTUVWXYZ1234567890!
@#$%^&*()_+";

        Random random = new Random();
        char[] password = new char[length];

        for (int i = 0; i < length; i++)
        {
            password[i] = validChars[random.Next(validChars.Length)];
        }

        return new string(password);
    }
}


// Music Playlist Manager Program in C#
using System;
using System.Collections.Generic;

class MusicPlaylistManager
{
    static List<string> playlist = new List<string>();

    static void Main()
    {
        while (true)
        {
            Console.WriteLine("Music Playlist Manager");
            Console.WriteLine("1. Add Song to Playlist");
            Console.WriteLine("2. View Playlist");
```

```csharp
        Console.WriteLine("3. Exit");

        Console.Write("Enter your choice: ");

        int choice = Convert.ToInt32(Console.ReadLine());

        switch (choice)
        {
          case 1:
            AddSongToPlaylist();
            break;
          case 2:
            ViewPlaylist();
            break;
          case 3:
            return;
          default:
            Console.WriteLine("Invalid choice. Please try again.");
            break;
        }
      }
    }

  static void AddSongToPlaylist()
  {
    Console.Write("Enter song name: ");
    string songName = Console.ReadLine();
    playlist.Add(songName);
    Console.WriteLine("Song added to playlist.");
  }

  static void ViewPlaylist()
  {
```

```csharp
        if (playlist.Count == 0)
        {
            Console.WriteLine("Playlist is empty.");
            return;
        }

        Console.WriteLine("Playlist:");
        foreach (string song in playlist)
        {
            Console.WriteLine(song);
        }
    }
}
```

Countdown to Events Program in C#

```csharp
using System;
using System.Threading;

class CountdownToEvents
{
    static void Main()
    {
        Console.WriteLine("Countdown to Events");
        Console.Write("Enter event date and time (MM/dd/yyyy HH:mm:ss): ");
        DateTime eventDateTime = DateTime.ParseExact(Console.ReadLine(),
"MM/dd/yyyy HH:mm:ss", null);

        TimeSpan remainingTime = eventDateTime - DateTime.Now;

        Console.WriteLine("Countdown started...");
        while (remainingTime.TotalSeconds > 0)
```

```
        {
            Console.WriteLine("Time remaining: " +
remainingTime.ToString(@"dd\.hh\:mm\:ss"));
            Thread.Sleep(1000);
            remainingTime = eventDateTime - DateTime.Now;
        }

        Console.WriteLine("Event time reached!");
    }
}


// Personal Diary Program in C#

using System;
using System.IO;

class PersonalDiary
{
    static void Main()
    {
        Console.WriteLine("Personal Diary");
        Console.Write("Enter diary entry: ");
        string entry = Console.ReadLine();

        WriteToDiary(entry);
        Console.WriteLine("Diary entry recorded.");
    }

    static void WriteToDiary(string entry)
    {
```

```csharp
    string diaryFilePath = "diary.txt";

    using (StreamWriter writer = new StreamWriter(diaryFilePath, true))

    {

        writer.WriteLine(DateTime.Now.ToString("MM/dd/yyyy HH:mm:ss") + ": " +
entry);

    }

  }

}
```

Morse Code Generator Program in C#

```csharp
using System;

using System.Collections.Generic;


class MorseCodeGenerator

{

    static Dictionary<char, string> morseCodeMap = new Dictionary<char, string>()

    {

        {'A', ".-"}, {'B', "-..."}, {'C', "-.-."}, {'D', "-.."}, {'E', "."},

        {'F', "..-."}, {'G', "--."}, {'H', "...."}, {'I', ".."}, {'J', ".---"},

        {'K', "-.-"}, {'L', ".-.."}, {'M', "--"}, {'N', "-."}, {'O', "---"},

        {'P', ".--."}, {'Q', "--.-"}, {'R', ".-."}, {'S', "..."}, {'T', "-"},

        {'U', "..-"}, {'V', "...-"}, {'W', ".--"}, {'X', "-..-"}, {'Y', "-.--"},

        {'Z', "--.."}, {'1', ".----"}, {'2', "..---"}, {'3', "...--"}, {'4', "....-"},

        {'5', "....."}, {'6', "-...."}, {'7', "--..."}, {'8', "---.."}, {'9', "----."},

        {'0', "-----"}, {' ', " "}

    };

    static void Main()

    {

        Console.WriteLine("Morse Code Generator");

        Console.Write("Enter text to convert to Morse code: ");
```

```csharp
    string text = Console.ReadLine().ToUpper();

    string morseCode = "";
    foreach (char c in text)
    {
      if (morseCodeMap.ContainsKey(c))
      {
        morseCode += morseCodeMap[c] + " ";
      }
    }

    Console.WriteLine("Morse code: " + morseCode);
  }
}


// Address Book with Database Program in C#
using System;
using System.Collections.Generic;

class AddressBook
{
  static Dictionary<string, string> contacts = new Dictionary<string, string>();

  static void Main()
  {
    while (true)
    {
      Console.WriteLine("Address Book");
      Console.WriteLine("1. Add Contact");
      Console.WriteLine("2. View Contacts");
      Console.WriteLine("3. Exit");
```

```csharp
        Console.Write("Enter your choice: ");

        int choice = Convert.ToInt32(Console.ReadLine());


        switch (choice)

        {

            case 1:

                AddContact();

                break;

            case 2:

                ViewContacts();

                break;

            case 3:

                return;

            default:

                Console.WriteLine("Invalid choice. Please try again.");

                break;

        }

    }

}


static void AddContact()

{

    Console.Write("Enter contact name: ");

    string name = Console.ReadLine();

    Console.Write("Enter contact number: ");

    string number = Console.ReadLine();


    contacts[name] = number;

    Console.WriteLine("Contact added successfully.");

}
```

```
  static void ViewContacts()
  {
    if (contacts.Count == 0)
    {
      Console.WriteLine("No contacts found.");
      return;
    }


    Console.WriteLine("Contacts:");
    foreach (KeyValuePair<string, string> contact in contacts)
    {
      Console.WriteLine("Name: " + contact.Key + ", Number: " + contact.Value);
    }
  }
}
```

Library Management System Program in C#

```
using System;
using System.Collections.Generic;
class LibraryManagementSystem
{
  static Dictionary<string, List<string>> library = new Dictionary<string,
List<string>>();
  static void Main()
  {
    while (true)
    {
      Console.WriteLine("Library Management System");
      Console.WriteLine("1. Add Book");
      Console.WriteLine("2. View Books");
      Console.WriteLine("3. Exit");
```

```csharp
        Console.Write("Enter your choice: ");

        int choice = Convert.ToInt32(Console.ReadLine());

        switch (choice)

        {

            case 1:

                AddBook();

                break;

            case 2:

                ViewBooks();

                break;

            case 3:

                return;

            default:

                Console.WriteLine("Invalid choice. Please try again.");

                break;

        }

    }

}

static void AddBook()

{

    Console.Write("Enter book category: ");

    string category = Console.ReadLine();

    Console.Write("Enter book title: ");

    string title = Console.ReadLine();


    if (!library.ContainsKey(category))

    {

        library[category] = new List<string>();

    }


    library[category].Add(title);
```

```csharp
      Console.WriteLine("Book added successfully.");

  }

  static void ViewBooks()

  {

    if (library.Count == 0)

    {

      Console.WriteLine("Library is empty.");

      return;

    }


    Console.WriteLine("Library Books:");

    foreach (KeyValuePair<string, List<string>> category in library)

    {

      Console.WriteLine("Category: " + category.Key);

      foreach (string title in category.Value)

      {

        Console.WriteLine("- " + title);

      }

    }

  }

}
```

Text Encryption/Decryption

```csharp
using System;

using System.IO;

using System.Security.Cryptography;

using System.Text;


class TextEncryptionDecryption

{

  static byte[] Encrypt(string plainText, byte[] key, byte[] iv)
```

```csharp
    {
        using (Aes aesAlg = Aes.Create())
        {
            aesAlg.Key = key;
            aesAlg.IV = iv;

            ICryptoTransform encryptor = aesAlg.CreateEncryptor(aesAlg.Key, aesAlg.IV);

            using (MemoryStream msEncrypt = new MemoryStream())
            {
                using (CryptoStream csEncrypt = new CryptoStream(msEncrypt, encryptor, CryptoStreamMode.Write))
                {
                    using (StreamWriter swEncrypt = new StreamWriter(csEncrypt))
                    {
                        swEncrypt.Write(plainText);
                    }
                    return msEncrypt.ToArray();
                }
            }
        }
    }

    static string Decrypt(byte[] cipherText, byte[] key, byte[] iv)
    {
        using (Aes aesAlg = Aes.Create())
        {
            aesAlg.Key = key;
            aesAlg.IV = iv;

            ICryptoTransform decryptor = aesAlg.CreateDecryptor(aesAlg.Key, aesAlg.IV);
```

```csharp
            using (MemoryStream msDecrypt = new MemoryStream(cipherText))
            {
                using (CryptoStream csDecrypt = new CryptoStream(msDecrypt, decryptor,
CryptoStreamMode.Read))
                {
                    using (StreamReader srDecrypt = new StreamReader(csDecrypt))
                    {
                        return srDecrypt.ReadToEnd();
                    }
                }
            }
        }
    }

    static void Main()
    {
        try
        {
            string plainText = "This is a secret message.";
            byte[] key = { 0x01, 0x02, 0x03, 0x04, 0x05, 0x06, 0x07, 0x08, 0x09, 0x0A,
0x0B, 0x0C, 0x0D, 0x0E, 0x0F, 0x10 };
            byte[] iv = { 0x01, 0x02, 0x03, 0x04, 0x05, 0x06, 0x07, 0x08, 0x09, 0x0A,
0x0B, 0x0C, 0x0D, 0x0E, 0x0F, 0x10 };

            byte[] encrypted = Encrypt(plainText, key, iv);
            Console.WriteLine("Encrypted Text: " + Convert.ToBase64String(encrypted));

            string decrypted = Decrypt(encrypted, key, iv);
            Console.WriteLine("Decrypted Text: " + decrypted);
        }
```

```
        catch (Exception ex)

    {

        Console.WriteLine("Error: " + ex.Message);

    }

  }

}
```

Barcode Generator

```
Install-Package ZXing.Net

using System;

using System.Drawing;

using ZXing;

class BarcodeGenerator

{

    static void Main()

    {

      try

      {

        // Create a barcode writer

        BarcodeWriter writer = new BarcodeWriter

        {

            Format = BarcodeFormat.CODE_128, // You can choose other barcode
formats as well

            Options = new ZXing.Common.EncodingOptions

            {

                Height = 100, // Height of the barcode (in pixels)

                Width = 300   // Width of the barcode (in pixels)

            }

        };
```

Mastering Practical C-Sharp Programming

```csharp
        // Generate the barcode image
        Bitmap barcodeBitmap = writer.Write("123456789"); // Enter your barcode content here

        // Save the barcode image to a file (optional)
        barcodeBitmap.Save("barcode.png",
System.Drawing.Imaging.ImageFormat.Png);

        Console.WriteLine("Barcode generated successfully.");
      }
    catch (Exception ex)
      {
        Console.WriteLine("Error: " + ex.Message);
      }
    }
}
```

Pomodoro Timer

```csharp
using System;
using System.Threading;

class PomodoroTimer
{
  static void Main()
  {
    int workDurationMinutes = 25;
    int breakDurationMinutes = 5;
    int pomodoroCount = 0;

    Console.WriteLine("Pomodoro Timer");
    Console.WriteLine("Press Ctrl+C to exit.");
```

```csharp
        try
        {
            while (true)
            {
                // Work interval
                pomodoroCount++;
                Console.WriteLine($"Pomodoro {pomodoroCount}: Work for
{workDurationMinutes} minutes.");
                RunTimer(workDurationMinutes);

                // Break interval
                Console.WriteLine($"Pomodoro {pomodoroCount}: Take a
{breakDurationMinutes} minute break.");
                RunTimer(breakDurationMinutes);
            }
        }
        catch (ThreadInterruptedException)
        {
            Console.WriteLine("Timer stopped.");
        }
    }

    static void RunTimer(int durationMinutes)
    {
        int durationSeconds = durationMinutes * 60;
        DateTime endTime = DateTime.Now.AddSeconds(durationSeconds);

        while (DateTime.Now < endTime)
        {
            Console.Write($"\rTime remaining: {endTime - DateTime.Now}");
```

```csharp
            Thread.Sleep(1000);

    }


    Console.WriteLine("\nTime's up!");

  }

}
```

www.ingramcontent.com/pod-product-compliance
Lightning Source LLC
LaVergne TN
LVHW020345200726
843507LV00012B/2497